HOLINESS FOR EVERYONE

St Francis de Sales' *Introduction to the Devout Life*

For Jannie Sayer
with gratitude

HOLINESS FOR EVERYONE

St Francis de Sales' *Introduction to the Devout Life*

Simplified and illustrated by
Elizabeth Ruth Obbard

New City

First published in 2016
in Great Britain by
New City

© 2016 Elizabeth Ruth Obbard

© Illustrated by Elizabeth Ruth Obbard

Graphic editor Sandy Bartus

British Cataloguing-in-Publication Data:
A catalogue record for this book is available from the
British Library

ISBN 978-1-905039-27-2

Typeset in Great Britain by
New City, London

Printed and bound by Gutenberg Press Ltd

CONTENTS

PART 3 – NECESSARY COUNSELS ABOUT VIRTUES AND VICES

PART 4 – COUNSELS ABOUT THE MOST USUAL TEMPTATIONS

PART 5 – EXERCISES AND INSTRUCTIONS FOR RENEWAL

INTRODUCTION

Saint Francis de Sales (1567–1622) was bishop of Geneva, a prolific letter writer, author, and co-founder with St Jane Frances de Chantal of the Order of the Visitation. These two initiated a new form of spirituality in the Church that has developed and borne fruit over many years. Salesian spirituality is noted for its stress on simplicity, openness to God, and a desire to make holiness accessible to all, no matter what vocation a person follows. Whether married or single, called to the religious life or priesthood, whether in politics or the military, or within the confines of home and family - all are invited to love God and live lives of holiness permeated with a spirit of gentleness and kindness towards all.

Francis was a much loved, first born child, gifted, intelligent, and obviously marked out for a brilliant career in whatever field he might choose. However, when studying in Paris he underwent a spiritual crisis over the question of predestination. Was it possible that God might reject him forever, despite the love he felt for him? Francis became ill with despair. He was saved by a radical abandonment to the mercy of a God who could be loved in the present moment. This offered freedom, hope and interior joy to the troubled young man.

As his studies continued at the university of Padua, Francis contemplated a career in law, coupled with private courses in theology. However, on returning home in 1592 at the age of twenty-five, he decided to become a priest rather than a lawyer, and after Ordination was assigned as assistant (or provost) to the bishop of Geneva.

At that time Geneva was in the hands of the Calvinists, and the bishop exercised his pastoral role from the town of Annecy, some fifty miles away.

Francis took up missionary work in the area, preaching and teaching the power of love and trying to incarnate it in his own life. He wanted persuasion to win rather than force. He was in contact with the greatest French minds of the time in their desire for reform in the Catholic Church. The new spiritual awakening saw people like Vincent de Paul, Madame Acarie, Pierre de Berulle and others seeking ways to bring holiness and social concern to the ordinary Christian.

Francis succeeded to the see of Geneva and within a short time met Jane Frances, Baroness de Chantal, who was a young widow with four small children. The sudden death of her husband in a hunting accident had left her grieving for many years. In her sorrow she discovered a deeper longing for God and felt that she would not marry again. Francis and Jane formed a deep bond of love and support; she encouraging him, he facilitating her inner growth and vocation to begin a new religious community, the Visitation of Holy Mary. This was an Order dedicated to prayer, but without the physical austerity of some of the newly reformed Orders like the Carmelites. A spirit of love, gentleness, simplicity was to be the hallmark of the Visitation. From now on Francis and Jane would be supportive equals as spiritual guides and reformers. Liberty of spirit was their watchword. Acting from love was more important than penitential exercises.

Francis was a man who understood human nature and wanted to see the best of the human virtues flourish. He wanted Jesus to live again in human beings, men and women, in whatever manner of life or strata of society they found themselves.

Writing, travelling, preaching, it was exhaustion that eventually killed Francis. He died of apoplexy in 1622, after meeting with Jane for the last time. Each had encouraged and supported the other, and they shared a vision of spirituality that was to endure, not only in the Orders they founded, but also in numerous spiritual offspring. For example, St John Bosco, who later founded his own Salesian Congregation, built his whole theory of education on the loving acceptance of the young (including troubled delinquents) and the nourishment of their humanity according to the precepts of Francis de Sales and Jane de Chantal.

Salesian spirituality, while radical in its demands, does not situate holiness in withdrawal and penance as does the early monastic tradition, with lay Christians trying to emulate as closely as possible the life of a monk or nun while remaining in the world. Francis offers a vision of holiness 'the devout life' to everyone, whether in the cloister or in the midst of secular affairs. Holiness is to blossom where one is planted, not in some rarified atmosphere. In the context of the daily round of prayer, work and leisure, God is to be found. God is present in marital relationships, in cordial affection, friendship and mutual respect for difference. Holiness is offered to everyone, because the love of Jesus is available to everyone.

Francis and Jane together lay stress on the small things of life that can make a difference. Salesian spirituality can accommodate not only those gifted in personality and temperament, but also those who must practice the more hidden virtues, and who struggle with difficulties of temperament and upbringing. There is room for all.

The classic termed 'Introduction to the Devout Life' began as a series of letters to one of Francis' spiritual daughters, Madame de Charmoisy, and a few others who looked to him for direction. It was first printed in 1608, but was so much in demand that other editions quickly followed, and Francis made his final revision of the text in 1619.

The book was immediately recognised as a masterpiece of mystical and devotional literature. Its appeal lies in its completeness, its originality, its balance and perfect harmony in setting forth the principles of holy living. Extremes are avoided. Holiness is made attractive and possible to everyone no matter what their vocation. Adaptations may be necessary, but the difference is not on a hierarchical scale. All are equally called to holy living, and Francis sets forth his arguments with warmth, charm and clarity.

A most loveable saint has written a classic that persuades by gentleness and love before all else. 'May Jesus live' was Francis' motto. His great desire was to see Jesus live in all men and women who came to him for direction. He wants to see Jesus live in each one who reads this book too, and he shows us how.

PART 1 – INSTRUCTIONS AND EXERCISES FOR ATTAINING THE GOAL OF LIVING A DEVOUT LIFE

What is Devotion?

You are seeking a life of devotion as a lover of God, so it is important to get the right idea from the start.

Real devotion makes us alert and alive in God's service and the love of our neighbour. It enables us to do good promptly and joyfully rather than with a long face and heavy heart. Love fans the flame of devotion into a great fire and enables us to run in the ways of God happily and agreeably.

People seem to have the idea that being religious is all about being gloomy, spending hours fasting and such like. But devotion adds sweetness to everything, just as the bee draws nectar from all kinds of plants and converts it into honey.

Devotion crowns love. It is as cream to milk, as flower to plant, as lustre to a precious stone, or perfume to balm. It comforts everyone who comes in contact with it. So seek it faithfully. You will not be disappointed.

Devotion is Suitable for All

Devotion isn't the same for everyone accross the board. It needs to be tempered to the specific calling of each one.

Is a married person supposed to live the life of a monk or nun? Should a bishop practice the poverty of a Franciscan? Should workers spend as much time in Church as those in ministry? Of course not!

Everyone is called to holiness according to their proper vocation, whatever it may be.

It is a mistake to think that holiness is only possible in the religious state. Not at all! In fact holiness makes every way of life more peaceful, pleasant, faithful and joyful.

We can see this in the saints of both Old and New Testaments. Some were married, some in the army, others attained holiness in their homes or in the service of their country.

Wherever we are and whatever our calling, we can and ought to seek perfection in a life of loving devotion.

Finding a Spiritual Companion for the Journey

It is good to go on the spiritual journey in the company of a good friend who will help us keep our focus.

Believe that such a friend is sent by God and be open and truthful in the search for such a person. We aren't able to go it alone. Good friends are God-friends.

A real friend for the journey is someone who should be full of love, knowledge and good sense. Without these gifts there is the possibility of being led astray.

Once you have found such a friend stay in their company and look no further. Your journey will be attended by every success.

The Necessity of Patience and Courage

The first steps in the way of holiness concern a healing of our former bad habits and sins.

Healing takes time. It is a gradual process, so we need to be patient and not expect perfection to come to us all at once.

Purification is a lifelong process. We may be wounded in the fight, so don't lose courage once you have set out on the spiritual path. Victory is assured for those who persevere.

Begin with a good confession, an overview of your whole life, and firmly resolve to live more fully for God.

Just resolving to get by with as little effort as possible is not a good sign! Free your heart and be joyful in giving. Those who go the whole way draw strength from their determination to hold nothing back.

Think how God has chosen you and loved you from the beginning. Think of the love of Jesus Crucified, his mercy and goodness; and so put the past behind you and give yourself unreservedly into the hands of the God who loves you so tenderly. In this way you will make a definitive break with your past sins and open yourself to a new future with confidence.

PUT YOURSELF IN GOD'S HANDS

Growing Towards the Light

As we grow in the gift of self, so we become more sensitive even to small faults. It is the result of the light of the Holy Spirit shining in our lives.

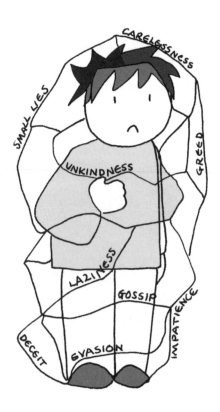

Any sin, even a small one, sullies us and weakens our devotion. We must, however, be specially on our guard against remaining attached to any sin, no matter how small it may seem to be.

Spiders do not kill bees, but they spoil the honey they make by spinning webs around the honeycomb, preventing the bees from carrying out their work with ease.

In the same way, small sins do not kill the soul, but they spoil our self-giving. They spin a web of bad habits around us, making it more difficult for us to practice love with the kind of zeal which we call devotion.

Telling a 'white lie', being careless in thought, word or action, overindulgence… Lapses like these are not important if we realise our mistake and turn back to God instantly. The danger lies in inviting and entertaining such faults over the long term. How could someone who loves God be content with a bad conscience and think things like this do not really matter? The honey of our devotion will quickly spoil if we entertain such an attitude.

Be generous and brave! It is easier in the long run.

Know yourself. Know your gifts. Know your bad tendencies. God wants the whole person that is you. Don't be content with anything less than this.

We are More than we Seem to Be

It is important to remember that you are God's creation and that you are made for more than this earth.

Give your life to God generously, remembering how God has blessed you, preserved you, called you to be his own.

Meditate on God's blessings, God's call, and the possibility of wasting the only life you have. Don't set your heart on things that pass: gourmet eating, expensive clothes, theatre going and such like. If you only think of earthly enjoyments and nourish yourself on what is ephemeral you'll get a 'fat soul', sluggish and unwilling to exert itself. Sit lightly on all that passes. Only children run after butterflies; adults are expected to pursue other more worthy goals!

Remember, no one is so good that they do not need to be circumspect, no one is so bad as to be past redemption.

PART 2 – VARIOUS INSTRUCTIONS CONCERNING PRAYER AND THE SACRAMENTS

On the Necessity of Prayer

There is nothing like prayer for opening our minds to the light of truth and our hearts to the warmth of God's love.

I specially recommend mental prayer, or prayer of the heart, particularly that which concerns meditation on the life and passion of Jesus. By looking at Christ you will come to understand him who is the light of the world, the well of living water which quenches our thirst.

By keeping close to Christ we gradually become like him in speech and action, just as children learn to speak by listening to and chattering to their mothers.

As glass in a mirror can never reflect anything unless the back be darkened, so we can never, by our own efforts, contemplate the Godhead apart from Jesus.

Jesus is the way to reach God the Father. He is the perfect mirror of the Divinity. Jesus calls himself the living bread; for as bread should be eaten with all kinds of foods, so Jesus should be our nourishment in all we do, pray and say.

I recommend spending an hour a day, preferably in the morning, in prayer.

Begin all prayer by placing yourself in the presence of God. This is a rule that you should keep to faithfully.

You will soon discover the profits that flow from it.

If for some reason you have not prayed in the morning, then try to do so in the afternoon. If neither choice is possible, then make up for it by doing some spiritual reading, saying many short prayers as you go about your work, or performing some act of self-denial. Meanwhile make a firm resolution not to miss your prayer time tomorrow. If you are drawn to mental prayer, then do not keep praying vocally but follow your attraction to silence. Don't try to fit in too many vocal prayers, be content with the Lord's prayer, the Hail Mary and the Creed. One Our Father, said well, is better than many said hastily and with a wandering mind.

A Method of Making Mental Prayer or Meditation

1)   Place yourself in the presence of God by calling to mind that God is present everywhere in creation, and present too in the depths of your soul.

Another way is to think of Jesus gazing upon you or being near you as a friend is near to another friend.

2)   Ask for God's help as you come before the Divine Presence, using a verse from a psalm, or asking one of the saints to inspire you according to what you intend to meditate on.

3)   Choose something from the gospels and bring it vividly to mind. Using your imagination helps to keep

unruly thoughts in check. But do this gently and without forcing yourself. Beginnners usually need some help like this to keep their focus.

4)	Spend time considering the mystery you have chosen, and stay with it as long as you are gaining light and help from it. Then move gently on without any undue haste. Draw honey from the same flower of prayer for as long as you can.

... MAKE ACTS OF LOVE

5)   Prayer made in this way should move us to make some further acts of love, such as putting into words a longing to be more like Jesus in our own lives, to grow in forgiveness, be more compassionate, and so forth.

Then be practical and concrete in making resolutions regarding your own life. Being content with vague generalisations about being better is not enough. Get down to basics.

6)   End your meditation by thanking God for all the inspirations you have received during your time of prayer. Then lay your life before God in union with the passion

and death of Jesus, and ask for all the graces you need for yourself and for the whole Church.

7) Lastly, gather a few thoughts to keep with you throughout the day, either before you leave your place of prayer or while walking about alone for a short time afterwards.

The fruit of prayer is a good life. Watch how you live and you will know how well you pray.

A last recommendation. If when you begin to pray you find your heart lifted effortlessly up to God in quietness and peace, then follow the movement of the Holy Spirit and forget all about a method.

A method is not to be slavishly followed but used as a support when needed. If it is not needed then just follow your heart with confidence in God's goodness and mercy.

When you have finished your prayer try to observe silence for a while as you return gently to your work. Do not get distracted, but be like someone carrying liquid in a precious porcelain vase. Any looking around might cause you to stumble, thus spilling the liquid. Learn to pass easily from prayer to work without losing the precious spirit of devotion.

Advice for when Prayer is Difficult

If at times prayer is dry and difficult, do not worry.
Say some vocal prayers.

Kiss the crucifix saying with Jacob 'I will not let you go unless you bless me' (Gen. 32: 26), or some similar verse from the Bible.

Another suggestion is to read a spiritual book quietly or make bodily prostrations if you are in a private place.

Above all do not become upset and worried. Just do what you can to remain quietly in God's presence.

We come to prayer for God, not ourselves.

Be patient. Give God the time you have resolved to give, and do it in whatever way you can. The results are God's business, not your own satisfaction.

Further Advice on Prayer

Beside your formal meditation, do not forget to pray every morning and evening for a short while. And above all, remain in the presence of God during the day.

In the morning remember that the day has been given you by God. Thank him for preserving you throughout the night, and try to forsee what the coming day may bring in the way of difficulties and their remedy. For example, if you think you will be speaking with a person easily angered, prepare yourself not to give offence, and also think of some pleasant words to keep the person sweet-tempered.

If you are to visit someone who is sick, think of when you will visit and the kind of help you can give graciously, and so forth. Then commend all to God, invoking our Lady and the saints to help you in your resolve.

In the same way, before supper, take some spiritual food by rekindling the fervour of your morning meditation and examining your conscience.

The birds have nests in the trees, the deer hide in thickets to enjoy coolness in the heat of summer. In the same way, our hearts should find somewhere to rest throughout the day: on Mount Calvary, in the wounds of Jesus, or in

some other place where we can find recollection and peace for a while, even in the midst of our daily work.

Make a shrine in your soul. Then, like St Catherine of Siena you can retire to it whenever you wish, and there speak to God, heart to heart.

Another practice is to have a fund of short prayers, bible verses, good thoughts, to fall back on when times are troublesome. Even the contemplation of nature can stir us to speak to God. Everything around us and about us should enable us to turn our thoughts Godwards.

Make use of this practice continually. You will find God present then at every turn.

Attend to good inspirations as they arise and nourish yourself on the Bible and other spiritual books, so that your mind is fed as well as your heart.

Make friends with the angels and saints. They are good companions for us and can help us on our way.

Especially think of the saint assigned to you in Baptism and whose name you bear.

Think of our Lady as a loving mother to whom you can run with confidence.

The spiritual journey is not made alone. We are surrounded by those who care for us and who can inspire us in so many ways.

We also help ourselves and others when we attend public prayers like the Divine Office.

Thoughts about Mass and the Sacraments

The Eucharist is the most important act of prayer, the greatest mystery of the Christian faith. Do all you can to be present at it every day.

Go to Confession regularly and be particular about examining yourself on how and why you sin.

Try to have a sincere sorrow for sin, and be straight and honest in looking at your motives as well as your actions.

When you receive Communion prepare yourself beforehand and make a fervent thanksgiving afterwards.

Jesus humbles himself to become our food. It is a time when he is most loving and tender, ready to heal and console those who approach him.

FEED YOUR MIND AS WELL AS YOUR HEART

By adoring and feeding upon beauty, purity and goodness in the Eucharist, you yourself will become beautiful, pure and good in your turn. Make yourself at home with the Eucharistic Lord and you will be transformed.

If you cannot be present at Mass in body because of other obligations, then try at least to be present in spirit. In the same way, if for some reason you cannot receive Holy

Communion, then make a spiritual communion in your heart.

The Eucharist is solid food. Receive it well. Receive it regularly.

PART 3 - NECESSARY COUNSELS
ABOUT VIRTUES AND VICES

Choosing virtues

When love enters our hearts, it always comes with other virtues in attendance, just as the queen bee is attended by all her little subjects when she goes into the fields. Virtues need to be exercised at appropriate times and in appropriate ways. The time of mourning and the time of gladness demand different responses.

We may not have many occasions to exercise fortitude, great heartedness and munificence in giving; but meekness, temperance, modesty and humility are qualities which are always in season. They may not be the rarest and greatest of virtues, but they are certainly the most universally necessary.

Along with the above we should practice the virtues that most accord with the kind of life we are called to live.

Look at the lives of the saints and you will see the different ways they found to live out their Christian calling: some through mercy to the poor, others through penance, others through preaching or welcoming pilgrims.

GIFTS

FAILINGS

LOOK IN THE RIGHT DIRECTION

Focus on your gifts and strong points rather than on your weaknesses and failures. That way you will make progress in the spiritual life, for one virtue practised perfectly brings others along with it.

It is a mistake to aim for perfection in such a way that harshness and severity predominate. Go gently and take advice from others. Growth is always gradual.

Exceptional gifts such as ecstasies, visions, raptures, are not virtues in themselves and are in no way necessary for the true service and love of God.

FOCUS ON JESUS

Concentrate on the virtues Jesus shows in his own life: patience, gentleness, obedience, poverty and so forth.

Better to be a good human being than a bad angel!

The Virtue of Patience

The more patient we are the more perfectly we are self-possessed and calm, not allowing ourselves to be shaken by troubles and contradictions, whether they come to us from good people or bad. In fact, it is harder to bear the criticisms of the good and a greater test of our forebearance.

Don't limit your patience to this or that kind of affliction, being willing to bear only such as seem honourable: being wounded in war for example, being persecuted for one's religious beliefs, losing money in a lawsuit in which one eventually wins out. In such cases people do not love suffering, but only the honour that goes with it.

The true servant of God bears up, no matter from what quarter criticism comes. Be ready to accept everything that God sends without picking and choosing.

Suffering can also come in the secondary circumstances that accompany the main problem. Being poor oneself is often not as painful as being unable to give gifts to friends. Slanders are more easily borne if one's friends do not believe the worst, while it is exceedingly painful if they do.

Learn to be patient when suffering comes your way, especially illness or inconveniences of one kind or another, no matter what may be their source.

Quit complaining! It does no good to you or anyone else! Learn to turn your gaze to Christ Crucified and see his own patience under suffering. Then you will get a better sense of proportion about your own troubles.

Inner and Outer Humility

To receive the gifts God wants to give us, our hearts must be emptied of all vainglory. Christ and his Mother are the greatest exemplars of humility. It is a virtue more prized by God than all the others.

Some people are proud because of the number of expensive possessions they have, or because of their physical beauty or superior education.

Riding a fine horse (or having an expensive car!), wearing a feather in one's cap (or a designer label in one's shirt!) are more to do with the the animal, the bird (and the manufacturer) than the one who possesses such things. They tell us nothing about the worth of the person at all.

The same goes for how we look or the talents we are endowed with. It is a mistake to seek after and overvalue such things. They are no indication of the goodness or otherwise of the person concerned. Material possessions are not wrong in themselves, but to think that our worth depends on them is to be gravely mistaken.

Real humility is interior. It does not mean denigrating ourselves, but thanking God for what we have been given and appreciating God's goodness and mercy towards us who so often fail. It is amusing to see people putting themselves down in conversation, then becoming furious if others agree that they are less than perfect!

Live truthfully, valuing yourself and your gifts, but not overvaluing them as if you were responsible for your own goodness.

Aim high, but do so with a realistic assessment of who you are and what you are called to be and become.

Be joyful and simple in your self-giving and go ahead with confidence. Gradually you will come to a realistic self-love even when life is challenging.

Embrace difficulties with a humble heart and they will soon taste sweeter than honey.

It is better to be good than to try and preserve a good name by endeavouring to please everyone. Reputation isn't everything. Reality is what counts.

The Virtue of Gentleness

Jesus calls himself 'gentle and humble of heart' (Matt. 11: 29). Humility perfects our relationship with God. Gentleness perfects our relationship with our neighbour.

It is like the chrism used in Confirmation, which is composed of olive oil mingled with balm. As our hearts are consecrated to Jesus so we should be like him in everything, mingling humility with gentleness.

Gentleness, peace, friendship should permeate all we do. Even if we have to correct someone we should never do so in an angry or violent manner. Anger is never justified. It can so easily turn into revenge or hatred of the other.

We should be gentle too with ourselves, eschewing all

harsh judgement of our sins and failings. Much better to be calm and peaceful. Any correction administered with gentleness is far more effective than one administered with passion or anger. We know that with respect to others. Let us apply the same yardstick to ourselves.

Avoidance of Over-eagerness and Anxiety

Worry is the bane of so many lives.

Rivers which flow gently through the plains carry large ships and rich merchandise, but rushing torrents were never suitable for shipping. In the same way work done hurriedly and impetuously is never well done.

Drones make more noise than bees but they only produce wax, not honey. Be a honey maker by your calm demeanour. Hold fast to God's hand as you work. You know the maxim 'More haste, less speed'. Do one thing at a time and you will do well.

Be like a sailor bound for port. Keep your eyes on the sky rather than the ocean. In this way God will work in you and for you, and your work will bring a blessing along with it.

Poverty, Chastity and Obedience

Obedience consecrates our hearts to God; poverty consecrates our material possessions, while chastity consecrates our bodies to God's service. These are like three branches of the spiritual cross we must carry, and here I am not talking of vowed religious but of all who live a serious Christian life.

Obedience is to live in harmony with the wishes and commands of others. It can either be voluntary or imposed.

We do not choose our parents, our political leaders, our bishops, but we are obliged to obey and respect them.

We can choose our spiritual advisors and as such we should choose wisely and obey willingly.

To live as if the world revolved around ourselves and our own desires is to live in disobedience and unrelatedness.

Obedience requires life's give and take with an attitude of respect towards all.

Chastity gives us purity of body and radiance of soul. It is necessary for everyone, married or single.

As sexual persons we need to be aware of our dignity as embodied beings and use our bodies in a way consonant with our calling.

A pure heart in a chaste body should be our aim.

Rest upon the pure heart of Christ, the Lamb of God, and you will be cleansed from all that could harm your soul's radiance.

Poverty consists in being content with what we have and not being jealous or envious of those who have more.

If you are rich use your possessions wisely and well, for all are equal in dignity if not in wealth.

Don't be attached to what you have, otherwise, if you lose it, you will lose your peace of mind too.

Poor people can be rich in love, just as rich people can be poor in spirit. So nobody needs to be a loser!

POOR IN SPIRIT   RICH IN LOVE

On Good and Evil Friendship

Friendship is about mutual love and sharing. Make sure your own friendships are built upon qualities of mind and heart, not just passing accomplishments, much less the excitement of empty flirtations, or even 'affairs'.

And do not use your friends for gain. Love them for themselves not for what they can give you.

A true friend loves what you love and shares what you value. A true friend is a gift from God to be received with gratitude.

Do not become embroiled in superficial relationships which sap your energy and lead nowhere. Sharing at a deep level is what constitutes real friendship. Go for the reality, not the mirage.

Jesus had special friends in Martha, Mary and Lazarus, so did the saints. It is not a sign of perfection to keep from

making friends. But be sure that your friendships are good and holy ones. Choose your own special friends wisely and they will help, not hinder you on your way to God.

If you find yourself embroiled in a friendship that takes you into evil paths don't waste time trying to disentangle yourself. Cut, break, tear yourself away. Don't compromise your integrity, and don't be someone who makes friends with an eye to their usefulness. That is self-seeking, not love.

Exercising Self-denial

In self denial do not begin with outward things such as what you wear or what you eat. Begin with the heart which is the seat of all our actions. What we do takes on the quality of the heart we have within us.

Give Christ first place in your heart then your actions will flow from a Christlike source. Stamp all you do with the name of Jesus. Jesus in your eyes, your mouth, your hands, your whole way of being.

Live no longer by your own life, but live with the life of Christ dwelling within you (Gal. 2: 20).

Giving you a few brief guidelines I would say: be moderate in all things. Treat the body with respect not harshness. Try not to be choosy about what you eat, but take simply whatever is offered you with a grateful heart.

In the same way with sleep: take what you need. If possible go to bed early and rise in good time to greet the day.

As to clothes, make sure they are clean and attractive. There is no virtue in looking unkempt. Be adorned above all with graciousness, dignity and a good name.

Remember that it is better to concentrate on the inward rather than the outward and you will not go wrong. God wants us to cherish and promote life, not abuse it - either in ourselves or in others.

Concerning Solitude and Community

We need both time alone and time with others.

If others visit you, be attentive and entertaining. That is what God wants.

If you are alone, then learn to live with yourself before you foist your company upon others.

Don't become addicted to company for company's sake, and avoid anyone who would lead you into evil.

Speak reverently of God at all times, but also reverently of others. Intending no harm is not enough.

Eschew words of mockery, of contempt, of scorn. Instead be relaxed, friendly and at ease with all.

Do not judge others. We can never know their motives; and being judgemental shows us to have bitter and resentful hearts. Look for the good in everyone and you will find it.

Be compassionate of the weakness and ignorance you may see about you. And if by chance you have to watch over the conduct of others because you are a parent of young children or in charge of other vulnerable people, do your duty lovingly and then go about your own business!

Above all, never pass on gossip or reveal the faults of others. It is so easy to mingle compliments with barbed remarks or indulge in cruel mimicry. We just do not know the hearts of others. We are all capable of change and growth, even the worst of us. We know this through our own experience, so we should give everyone the benefit of the doubt and keep silent about any faults and sins we may notice.

Speak always gently, truthfully, sincerely and transparently. Candour is a beautiful trait in a person. It eschews anything underhand and makes us a pleasure to be with.

Be faithful to God always and God will be faithful to you. Be just. Be merciful. Desire to be the best you can be and give God your heart. The rest will follow naturally.

About Games and Recreational Activities

We need to relax both mind and body, otherwise we become taut like the string on a hunter's bow.

Walking, friendly conversation, playing a musical instrument, singing, riding, are all innocent recreations that we should make use of from time to time.

Those games which demand dexterity of body or mind, such as tennis or chess should also be used with moderation or they will become addictive. Addictive behaviour exhausts rather than refreshes.

Enjoy your enjoyments, but in such a way that they do not become the be all and end all of your life.

Gambling in any form is not recommended. All games of chance depend on the pleasure of winning. There is no joy in the faces of gamblers.

Parties and dances are not wrong in themselves. But watch yourself when dances go on late into the night. Turning night into day deprives you of a good morning given to God.

If you must go to dances go well prepared.

Dress yourself with modesty, comport yourself with

dignity. Dances are like mushrooms in my opinion, even the best are not much good, so partake of them sparingly.

After a party or dance make use of good and holy thoughts, and examine your conscience on how you behaved while there. Like all things, dancing and partying are good in moderation, so make up your own mind on the subject.

St Elizabeth of Hungary enjoyed dancing without losing any of her deep rooted devotion. The fire of love in her heart was so strong that it increased rather than diminished when exposed to social occasions that could well have left others spiritually bereft.

A small fire is easily extinguished, while a great blaze thrives on a strong wind.

Advice on Care in Little Things

Do not be careless about little things, but be like the valiant woman who put her hand also to strong things (Prov. 31: 19). Exercise yourself in great love while never forgetting the humble virtues.

Great occasions to serve God are infrequent, so make the most of the many small occasions that come your way.

Whether you eat or drink, whether you sleep of recreate, cook or dance, do all for God.

Live according to the vocation God has given you rather than envying the calling of others. Contentment lies in loving what we have, not craving what we cannot have.

Every calling has its blessings and crosses. Embrace your own particular vocation and live it well. That is the way to happiness.

Advice to the Married

Jesus attended the wedding of Cana. May he be present at every marriage so that the wine of consolations and blessings may never be lacking.

If you want a happy marriage consider the fact that marriage is a Sacrament of holiness and fosters a holy way

of life, consisting in mutual love and self giving.

The effect of this love is a union of hearts so strong that even the strongest glue cannot be compared with it. Another effect is inviolable mutual faithfulness, symbolised in the giving of rings.

The fruit of marriage is the blessing of children, images of God as well as of their parents.

True marital respect and intimacy fosters freedom for each partner rather than the desire to control the other, or give way to jealousy.

Many saints were married, giving one another mutual support and comfort. Real holiness is possible for the married as well as for the single and those vowed to religious life. Value your own vocation and find in it a true path to holiness.

What path you follow is not as important as what kind of heart you have and your capacity for love and forgiveness.

If widowhood comes, then consider whether you are called to a life of celibacy.

If you are a virgin, then keep your heart pure for the Lord, don't just take God as a 'second best' when all else has failed.

PART 4 – COUNSELS
ABOUT THE MOST USUAL TEMPTATIONS

The Dangers of Human Respect

When people see you beginning to live a serious Christian life they will no doubt object and think you have gone crazy. But they do not consider such things as spending whole days in games and empty amusements as crazy at all - pastimes that seem pretty dull to me.

Spending thirty consecutive nights partying is considered fine by some. Spending a night in prayer or getting up

early to go to Mass is thought of as meriting a visit to the doctor's surgery! Everything depends on the angle we are coming from.

So don't live your life by what other people think. Do what you believe to be right and take no notice of the judgements of others. We can never please everyone.

Have courage and patience. Bright light dazzles the eyes if you have lived a long time in darkness. You may have to take time to accustom yourself to life with Christ.

At first it may seem hard to continue in God's way, but gradually you will be filled with sweetness and joy if you persevere. Ultimately it gives us more happiness if we serve God rather than follow the standards of the world.

Grow strong through feeding on the honey of God's Word. Soon you will be able to fly. Ask God to give you the wings you need.

The Reality of Temptation

Being tempted, however long temptation continues, cannot make us displeasing to God. There is no blame attached to being tempted, as we see in the lives of the saints who all had their struggles. The secret is to take no pleasure in anything contrary to the will of God. In that way you will conquer.

Take the example of a princess, loving and beloved of her husband. She receives a letter from an admirer tempting her to commit adultery. The proposal is received. Either she likes the idea or not. Then she either consents or not.

We cannot always avoid temptation, but we can give or refuse our consent. Sometimes it will seem that the fire of our love for God is overlaid by the ashes of temptation,

with the love of God barely a tiny spark underneath. But do not give up. Refuse consent and you will come out triumphant even if battered.

What you really want will make itself known in the end. You may not feel good, but you will act rightly, and that is what counts.

Words of Encouragement

God allows us to be tempted because temptations strengthen us and help us to grow.

When tempted remain humble and do not rely on your own strength to win the victory. As long as a person's heart is beating we know that life continues in the body even if he or she remains unconscious. In the same way we should

EXAMINE YOUR HEART

examine our heart to see if we have consented to temptation, and if not, then we must know that Jesus the Saviour is with us, even if we are unconscious of his presence.

But watch that you are not the cause of temptation to yourself. Watch the kind of friends you make, the company you keep, the things you think about.

When you are tempted, then run for your life, like children who see a wolf or a bear and make straight for their parents' arms.

Don't waste time reasoning with temptation; give it no place at all to take root. Fill your mind and heart with good things instead, and tell someone you trust about what troubles you. Two heads are better than one when it comes to putting up a strong resistance.

Small Temptations

We have to fight great temptations with courage, but there is a special courage involved in resisting small temptations.

Wild animals are frightening and we run from them. Flies are smaller but they are a perpetual annoyance and try our patience to the utmost.

Remember that the Lord looks at the heart rather than the act. You may not have done anything really wrong, but your heart has given way perhaps to envy, jealousy, lying,

DISREGARD SMALL
ANNOYANCES

MAKE ACTS OF LOVE FOR GOD
INSTEAD

insincerity. These things need to be acknowledged and taken seriously. Being just 'good enough' is not good enough if you want to belong completely to God!

As with flies that flutter around and sometimes settle on our face, so with small temptations; the best way to get rid of them is to take no notice of them and instead make acts of love for God. Acts of love for God are the best weapon we have. Thus we will foster inner peace and calm.

Don't waste time over what is not worth wasting time over. Turn your heart to God and consider the rest as worthless.

On Anxiety

Being anxious is the bane of some people's lives. Anxiety is a waste of time and the cause of much sadness.

Of course we do not want to be faced with evils such as poverty, illness, contempt, dryness in prayer. But being anxious about these things does us no good at all.

Rather than giving in to anxiety be patient, humble, peaceful. Look for deliverance, trusting in God's goodness and providence rather than in your own hard work and worry.

The more we worry the more we weaken ourselves. We just get more and more discouraged and sad and then find it even harder to act.

When you want to be rid of some fault go about it gently and tranquilly. Gently does not mean that you do not use your God given energy, but it does mean going about things without over-anxiety and needless distress.

Relieve the pressure by talking to some good friend about what bothers you. That may well help to put everything in a better perspective.

TALK THINGS OVER WITH A FRIEND....

On Sadness

Sadness may be good or evil according to what it does to us. Good effects of sadness are compassion and repentance. Bad effects are anxiety, discouragement, anger, jealousy, envy and impatience. So you see that the bad effects outnumber the good!

The devil likes to see us sad and despondent about our efforts to grow in the love of God. We become like the earth in winter - hard, paralysed, cold. When this happens warm yourself at the fire of prayer. From it you will draw strength to do good works. Sing as you work! The devil hates 'singing souls' who are happy and strong.

Continue to do good even though you may not feel like it. Receive Communion regularly. Discuss your sadness with a wise director. And above all, trust that in good time God will take away your sadness and give you joy.

On Consolation and Desolation

Creation has been ordained by God to be in a continual state of flux: times and seasons alternate just as our moods and feelings do.

No matter what we may feel we must learn to keep our eyes fixed on God and our hearts steadfast in doing God's will. Devotion isn't about feeling good or enjoying prayer. It's about doing what God wants. Some people can feel great tenderness when they consider the Lord's sufferings, yet when their actions are put to the test they fail miserably.

A child will weep to see its mother sick, yet, if the same mother asks to be given the sweet or chocolate the child likes, she is refused! That's how we are with God. We want to hold on to our faults and sins even while we weep for the sufferings of Jesus on the cross.

At other times God does give us true feelings that stimulate us to do good and make other pleasures seem trifling. But we should never count ourselves to be better because of them. Above all we should want to do God's will.

When times are hard and prayer is difficult, hold on to the resolutions made in happier times. Prayer will sometimes be hard going. All the more reason then to persevere

in order to show God that you want God and not God's gifts.

Holiness consists in wanting what God gives us, not in wanting what we ourselves have decided is good for us. Love what you are given whether it be sweet or bitter to the taste. Then you will know what it is to be always joyful.

When you feel desolation or dryness, examine yourself on your behaviour. Have you been neglecting God? Have you been open with your confessor? Have you been careful to preserve the fruits of consolation?

If we discover that we are at fault then thank God for giving us light on the subject. Meanwhile call upon God for comfort and strength, and never lose heart. Continue your journey with patience. Feelings of sweetness are not necessary. Doing God's will is.

A Story by Way of Example

Many beginners become despondent when the way becomes hard. This story is drawn from the life of St Bernard and concerns one of his companions, Geoffrey of Peronne.

Geoffrey had lately dedicated himself to God's service, but when he underwent a period of spiritual darkness his thoughts returned to all he had recently left: family, friends, possessions... One of his companions noticed Geoffrey's sadness and asked for an explanation.

Geoffrey replied with a deep sigh that he would never be joyful again. Then overcome with sorrow he rested his head on a stone and fell asleep.

Meanwhile his friend had gone to tell St Bernard, and the saint betook himself to prayer.

When Geoffrey awoke he felt so happy as a result of Bernard's prayer that his friend was surprised at such a sudden and great change in him. He reminded Geoffrey of his previous lament that he would never be joyful again. Yet now Geoffrey only replied 'If I told you before I would never be happy again, now I tell you that I will never again be sad.'

You can see from this story that there are a number of lessons to be learned.

1)   God often gives a foretaste of delights to those who enter his service so as to make divine love attractive. Like a mother who puts honey on her breasts to make them pleasant for her infant.

2)   That the same good God sometimes decides to withold milk and honey, so that we may become accustomed to more dry and solid bread rather than sweetness alone.

3)   That sometimes great storms arise when we are dry and disconsolate. At such times we must bravely fight such temptations (since they are not from God) while patiently suffering the aridity and growing in virtue.

4)   We must never lose courage. Nor be like that Geoffrey who thought he would never again be joyful, and then that he would never again be sad. Life changes and we change with it, no matter the weather. Be humble, knowing that nothing remains unchangeable here on earth.

5)   Discuss your troubles with a spiritual friend who may be able to offer comfort.

God wants to lead us to purity of heart and disinterestedness in his service. The evil one wants to make us lose courage and return to our old ways.

Occasionally distaste and dryness flow from bodily sources such as excessive tiredness. The remedy is not to cease from doing the good we can. We should try to restore our bodily health so as to strengthen our spirit as well.

PART 5 - EXERCISES AND INSTRUCTIONS FOR RENEWAL

Annual Renewal of One's Resolution

Every year we should renew our good resolutions. It is very easy to become careless and that has fatal results.

A good watchmaker resets and rewinds a clock morning and evening. He also takes it apart every year and oils it thoroughly. So we should be careful to pray morning and evening, and anoint our hearts regularly with the oil of Confession and Communion.

When you have chosen a convenient time to renew your annual self gift to God take time to be alone and make the following considerations.

1)   That you have dedicated yourself completely to the love and service of God, and that you are resolved to forsake all sin.

2)   Consider that you have given God your word and so should be doubly faithful, even more so than if you had given your word to a human being.

3)   Consider in whose presence you have made your offering: the whole court of heaven with the angels and saints in attendance. As they rejoiced at your first offering, so now make them joyful that you are renewing it with fervour.

4)   Remember how grace invited you to live for God; and how you were led by divine sweetness and the impulses of love and charity.

5)   Remember that it was in youth that God called you, and what happiness it is to give God one's life from an early age. And if you were called when older thank God that you were called before life ended.

6)   Think what a blessing it is to belong to God. Compare what you are now to what you were before you began to walk this path, and be grateful for so many blessings.

Examination of Soul

Make a thorough annual examination of conscience, lasting over a period of time.

This can take place while walking or resting in bed, but be sure to keep from drowsiness and be aware of the points you are to consider beforehand.

Then place yourself in God's presence and consider how you stand in regard to serious sin.

Have you kept the Commandments?

Are you careful to avoid even small sins?

Are you regular with your spiritual exercises and how do you feel about them?

How are you in your dealings with God? Do you delight in remembering him? Do you want to love him more and more?

How is your relationship with Jesus Christ? Is he your happiness and the honey of your soul?

How are you in regard to our Lady and the saints? Do you love them fervently, confident in their patronage?

How do you use your tongue? Do you love to speak of God and sing God's praises?

In your works are you zealous for God's glory?

Have you given up anything for God's sake? To be able to give up something for love of another is a sign that love is true and strong.

On Loving Yourself

Consider how you love yourself.

Are you more concerned about material blessings and goods or about heavenly ones?

Are you willing to be patient with yourself and your weaknesses?

And how about your love of others? Don't just think about how you love those who love you, but how you behave towards those you love least. That will tell you how real your love is.

What makes you happy or sad? joyful or despairing? What do you love or hate?

By examining ourselves in these areas we can see what kind of music is being played in our life as a whole.

Drawing Everything Together

After you have considered all these points thank God for all God has done for you. Ask pardon for failures and promise to grow in faithfulness.

Give God your heart whole and undivided.

Consider the example of the saints and resolve to grow in holiness.

Build up your self respect, knowing yourself to be a valuable person, loved and redeemed. Long with an ever greater longing to grow in holiness. Goodness is its own reward, making you a more loveable person, more

content with who you are, more able to surmount troubles and difficulties. You can see examples of this in the lives of the saints.

An expectant mother prepares a cradle for her child and gets everything ready to receive the new life with love. So Jesus on the cross, wanting to bring you forth to salvation, has prepared all that you need to grow in holiness and happiness.

Seeing yourself so loved, your only response must be to love Jesus in return, the Jesus who 'loved me and gave himself for me' (Gal. 2: 20).

Growing in holiness is being resolved to bear fruit like a beautiful tree, planted by God in your heart and watered by the precious blood of the Saviour.

So take practical steps to live out your resolutions, such as saying short prayers throughout the day which continually redirect your heart Godwards.

Perseverance is a gift and a joy to those who keep going. Be one of those and you will face death with equanimity.

May Jesus reign, to whom, with the Father and the Holy Spirit, be honour and glory now and forever. Amen.

FOR FURTHER READING

Texts

Michael Day C.O. (Transl.): *Saint Francis de Sales - Introduction to the Devout Life,* Burns & Oates, London, 1956

De Sales F. & de Chantal F.: *Letters of Spiritual Direction, Classics of Western Spirituality,* (P. M. Thibert, VHM Transl.) Paulist Press, New Yersey, 1988

Related Works

Camus, J.P.: *The Spirit of St Francis de Sales,* (Trans & edited by John K. Ryan) Longmans, Green and Co., London, 1953

Cox M.: *A Handbook of Christian Mysticism,* The Aquarian Press, Wellingborough, 1986

Downey M.: *Understanding Christian Spirituality,* Paulist Press, New Jersey, 1997

Dupre L. & Saliers D.E. (ed.): *Christian Spirituality Vol III, Post Reformation & Modern*, SCM Press, Norwich, 1989

Ranft P.: *Women & Spiritual Equality in Christian Tradition*, St Martin's Press, New York, 2000

Trouncer M.: *The Gentleman Saint, St Francois de Sales and his Times*, Hutchinson & Co., London, 1963

Underhill E.: *Mysticism*, (12th Edition) New American Library, New York, 1974

Other books published from the Author

A Taste of Hildegard
ISBN: 9781905039173 - PB - pp 90

Gospel Childhood
ISBN: 9780904287943 - PB - pp 94

Introducing Julian, Woman of Norwich
ISBN: 9781905039142 - PB - pp 142

Life in God's Now
ISBN: 9781905039111 - PB - pp 81

Medieval Woman Mystics
ISBN: 9781565482784 - PB - pp 158

Our Father St Benedict
ISBN: 9781905039067 - PB - pp 127

Poverty - Simplicity - Joy
ISBN: 9781905039258 - PB - pp 111

St Teresa's Way of Perfection for Everyone
ISBN: 9780904287783 - PB - pp 93

The Cloud Of Unknowing For Everyone
ISBN: 9780904287974 - PB - pp 88

The Living Flame of Love
ISBN: 9780904287882 - PB - pp 82

Travelling Inwards
ISBN: 9781905039210 - PB - pp 89

Visit our online bookstore: www.newcity.co.uk